KJOS MULTIPLE OPTION SCORING

A BEST IN CLASS SHOWCASE

by Bruce Pearson and Chuck Elledge

Dear Student,

Welcome to **A BEST IN CLASS SHOWCASE**! Inside you will find ten exciting new band arrangements, written especially for beginning instrumentalists. But these aren't ordinary band arrangements. The music in this book lets **you** decide how to best display your new-found talents. Using our "multiple-option scoring" system, you can perform by yourself or with any size group you want. Play solos with a piano accompanist, play duets with your teacher, or get together with a group of friends—any number or combination of instruments! Like **A BEST IN CLASS CHRISTMAS**, this book is designed to provide years of musical learning and fun. We sincerely hope you enjoy this new collection, and, remember, always strive to do your best.

Best wishes,

Bruce Pearson

Chuck Elledge

© 1989 Kjos West, Neil A. Kjos Music Company, Distributor
4380 Jutland Drive, San Diego, California 92117
International copyright secured. All rights reserved. Printed in U.S.A.
WARNING! These compositions are protected by copyright law. To copy or reproduce them by any method is an infringement of the copyright law. Anyone who reproduces copyrighted matter is subject to substantial penalties and assessments for each infringement.

ISBN 0-8497-8396-8

Kjos Neil A. Kjos Music Company · San Diego, California

KJOS MULTIPLE OPTION SCORING

KJOS MULTIPLE-OPTION SCORING

Kjos Multiple-Option Scoring was invented to allow **you** to perform this music any way you like. You can perform alone, with a friend, or together with any number or combination of instrumentalists (with or without piano or guitar accompaniment). With Multiple-Option Scoring, you have the flexibility to design your own solo recital, group recital or full band concert. The arrangements are there to assemble however you choose!

ABOUT YOUR CLARINET BOOK

Each piece in this book contains four separate parts: [Melody], [A], [B], and [C]. The parts have a specific purpose, depending upon the performance situation:

Solos When playing a solo with piano or guitar accompaniment, play the [A] part. This part gives you the melody most of the time, with a few scattered rests for breathing room. If you are playing a solo without accompaniment, play the [Melody] part to eliminate the rests and put you in the spotlight throughout.

Duets When playing duets, one player should play the [A] part, and the other player should play the [B] part. If you are performing with another clarinet player, you can both read from this book. If your duet partner plays a different instrument, they should play the [A] or [B] part printed in the **BEST IN CLASS SHOWCASE** book for their own instrument. Duets can be played with or without piano/guitar accompaniment.

Larger Groups You can also form larger groups playing any combination of parts. Your book, for instance, contains a [C] part. The trombone, tuba, and low instrument books contain a [D] part, and the french horn book contains a [Special] part written just for them. Playing all of these parts together, you can create an almost infinite number of ensembles!

Full Band When these arrangements are played by a full band, your director will tell you which part to play. As a clarinet player, you may be called upon to play either the [A], [B], or [C] part in your book. Your band director will decide what best fits your full band.

In addition, the book for percussionists contains special drum parts, and the piano/guitar book contains accompaniments for all ten arrangements. Adding these parts to your ensembles creates an even greater variety of sounds.

If you are having difficulty with some notes, a fingering chart has been printed on the inside front cover. There are also some scale studies on the inside back cover. Practice these regularly to improve your technique.

Contents

Fingering Chart	Inside front cover
Billboard March	4
The Conquering Hero	6
BINGO!	8
Simple Gifts	10
Las Chiapanecas	12
Manhattan Beach	14
Minuet	16
Ricochet Rock	18
Hatikvah	20
When the Saints Go Marching In	22
Performance Notes	24
Scale Studies	Inside back cover

Billboard March

John N. Klohr

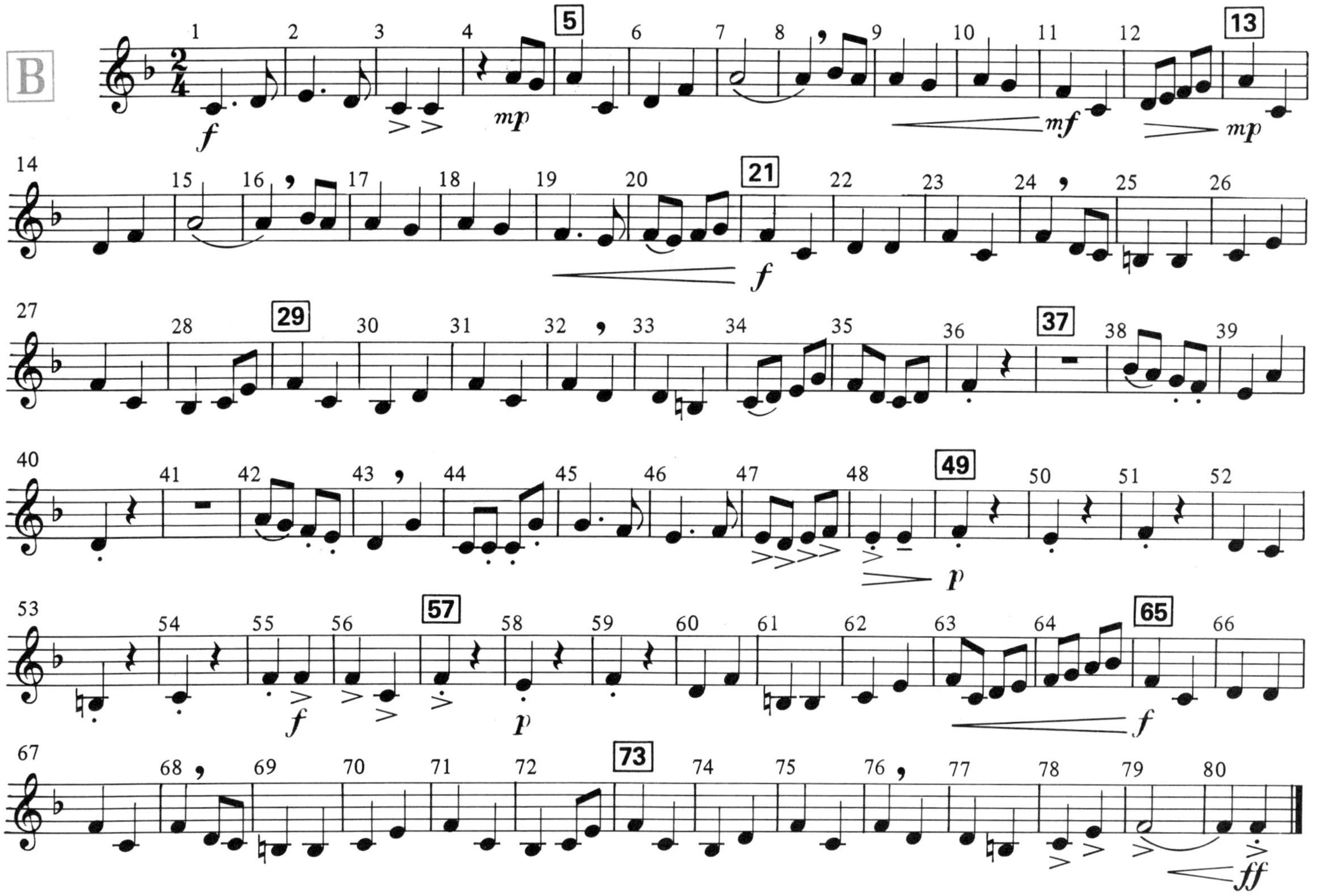
B

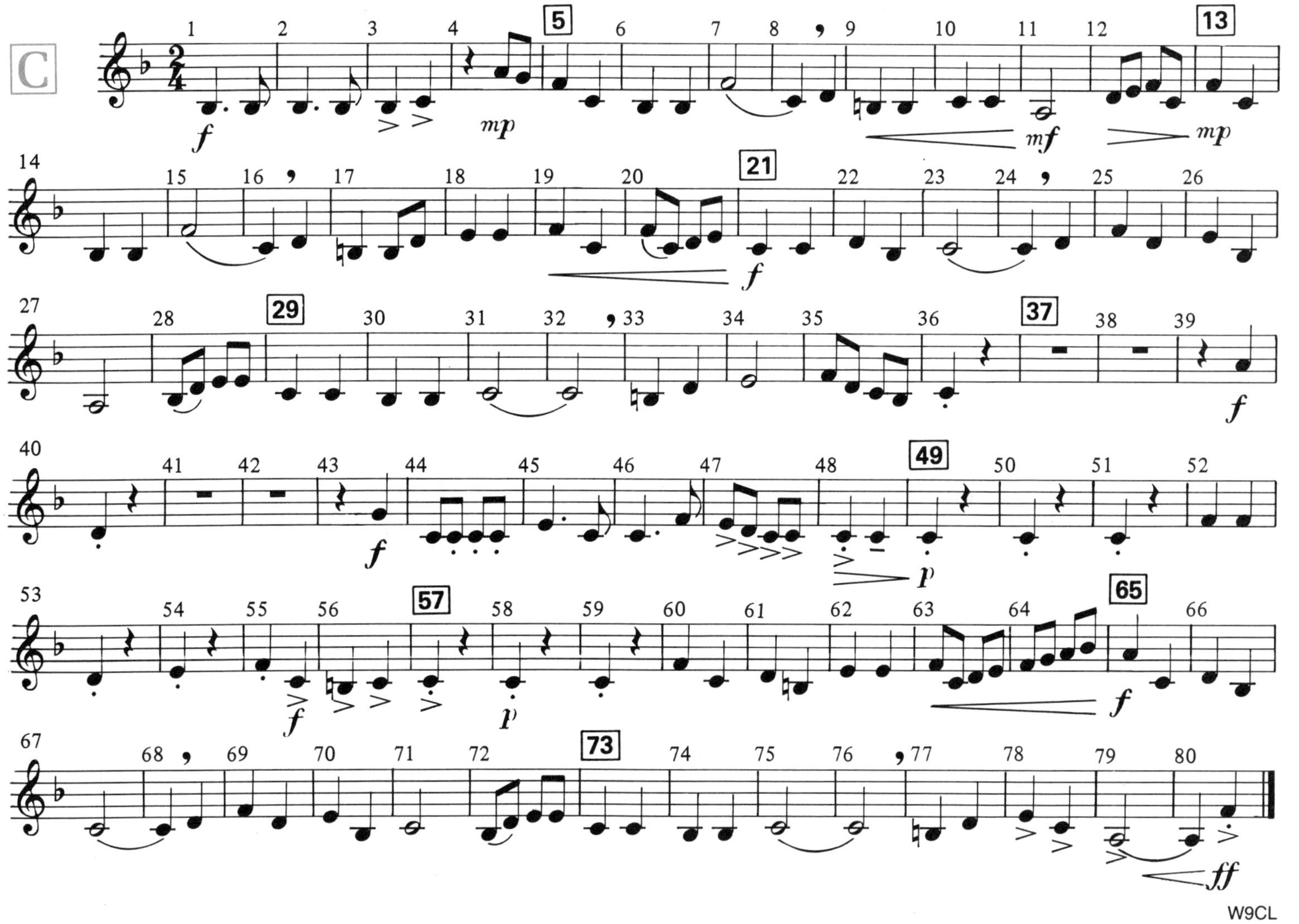
C

The Conquering Hero

G.F. Handel

B

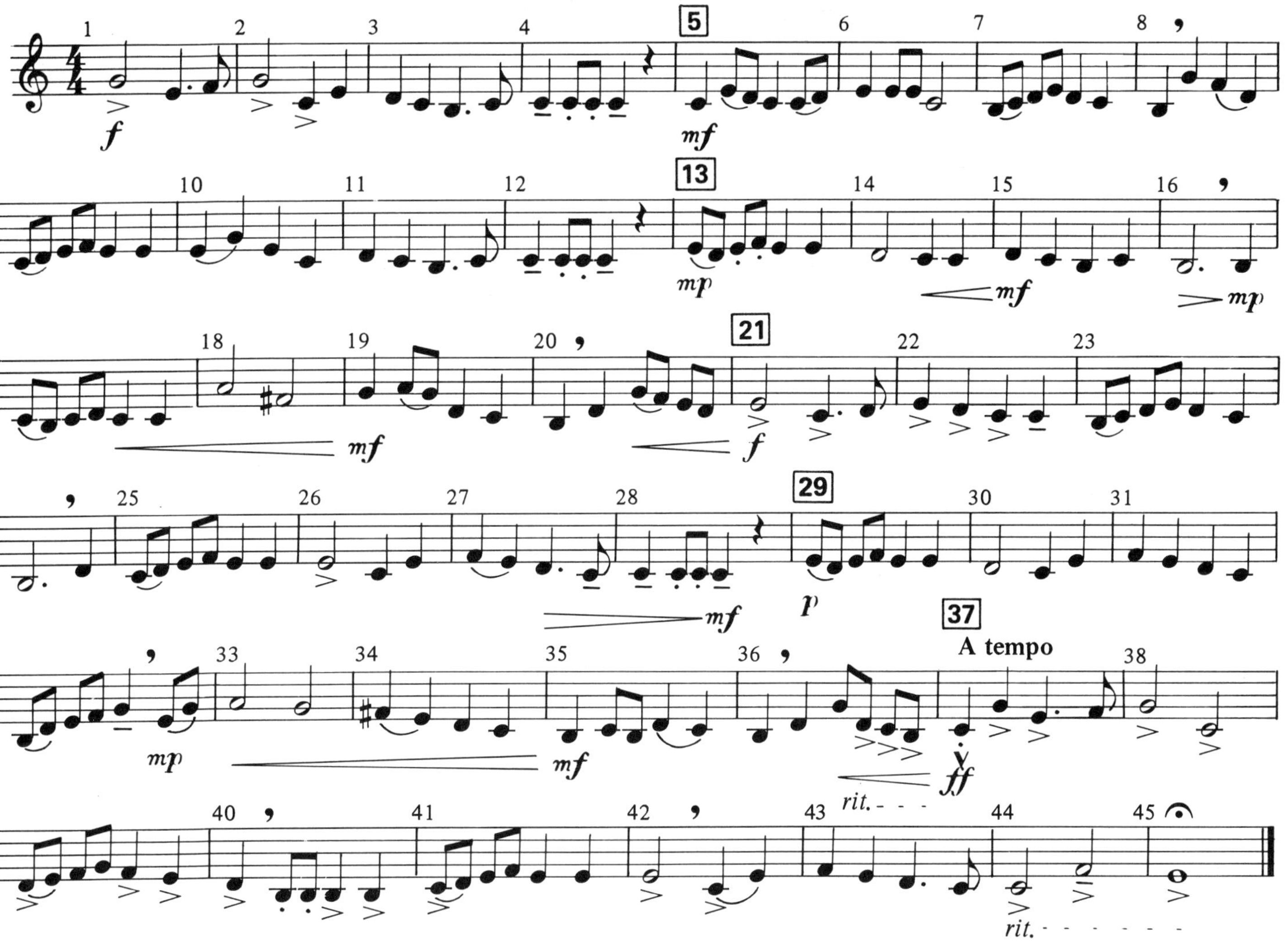

C

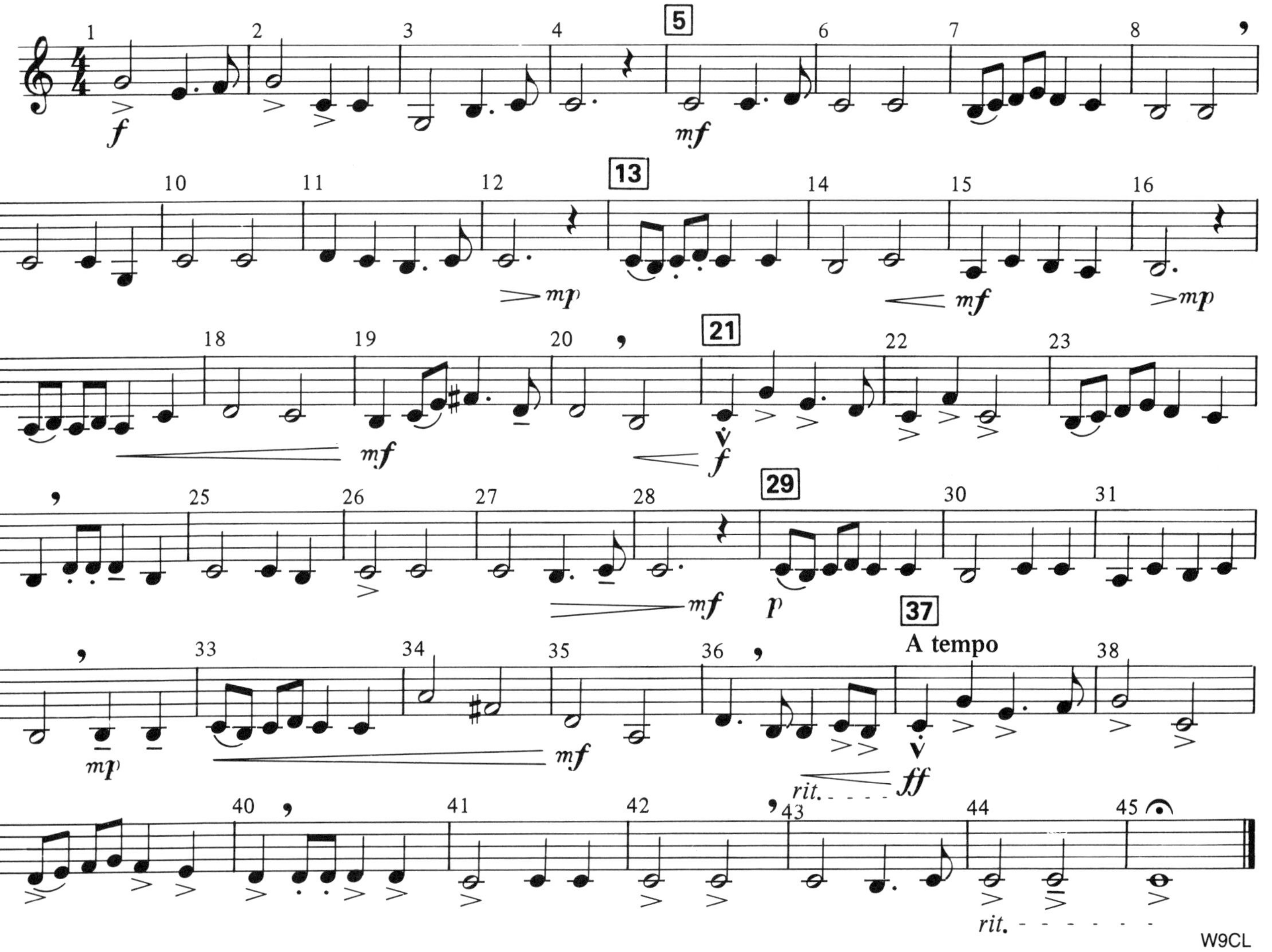

BINGO!

Folk Song

B
Foot Stomp
Yell or Sing
F.S.
B - I - N-G-O
Play
Yell or Sing
Bin-go!

C
Foot Stomp
Yell or Sing
F.S.
B - I - N-G-O
Play
Yell or Sing
Bin-go!

Simple Gifts

Shaker Melody

B
p
mp
p
mp
mf
mp
p
f
A tempo
mf
f
rit. - - -
mp
mf
ff
molto rit.

C
p
mp
p
mp
mf
mp
p
f
A tempo
mf
f
rit. - - -
mp
mf
ff
molto rit.

Las Chiapanecas

Mexican Folk Song

B

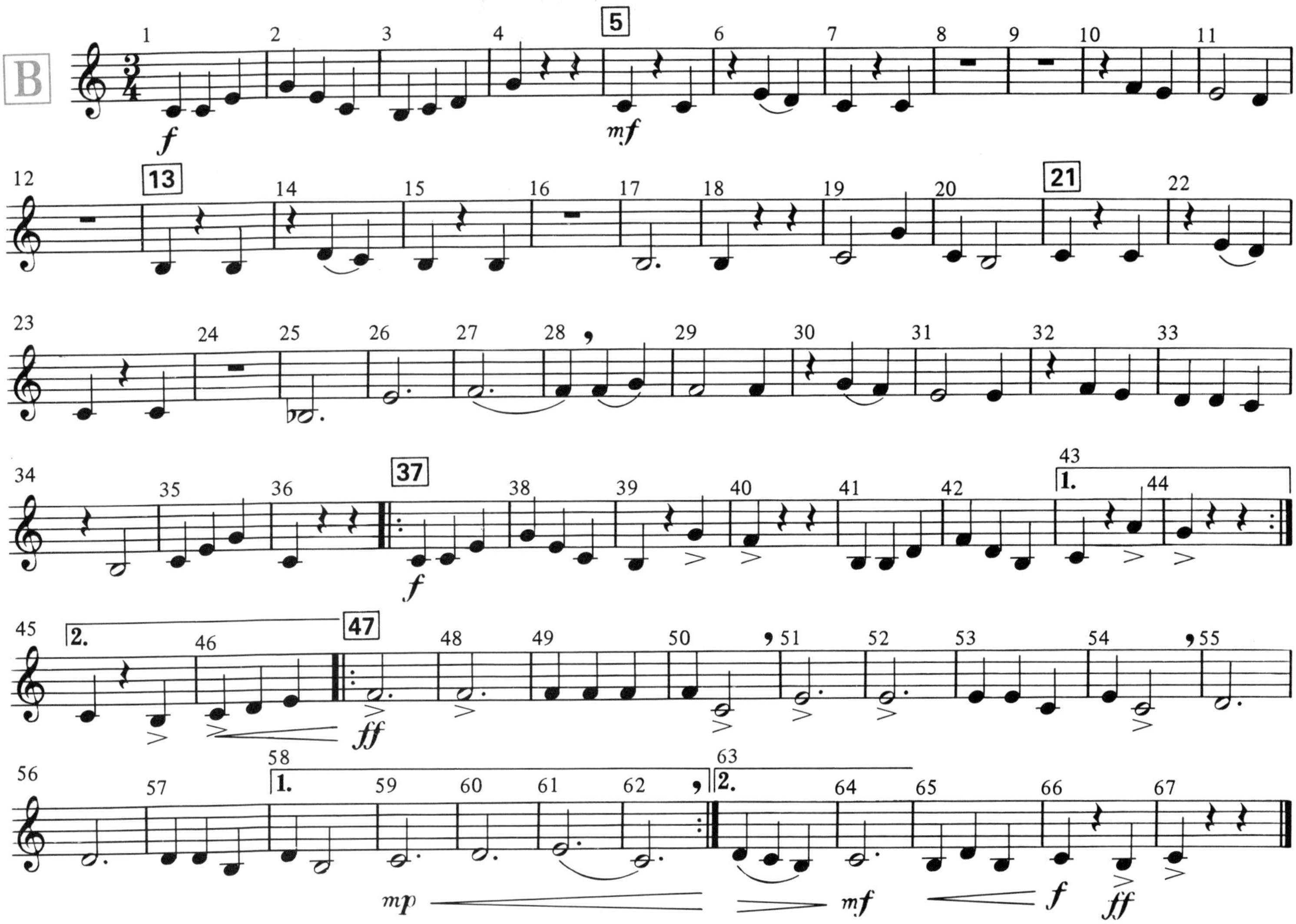

C

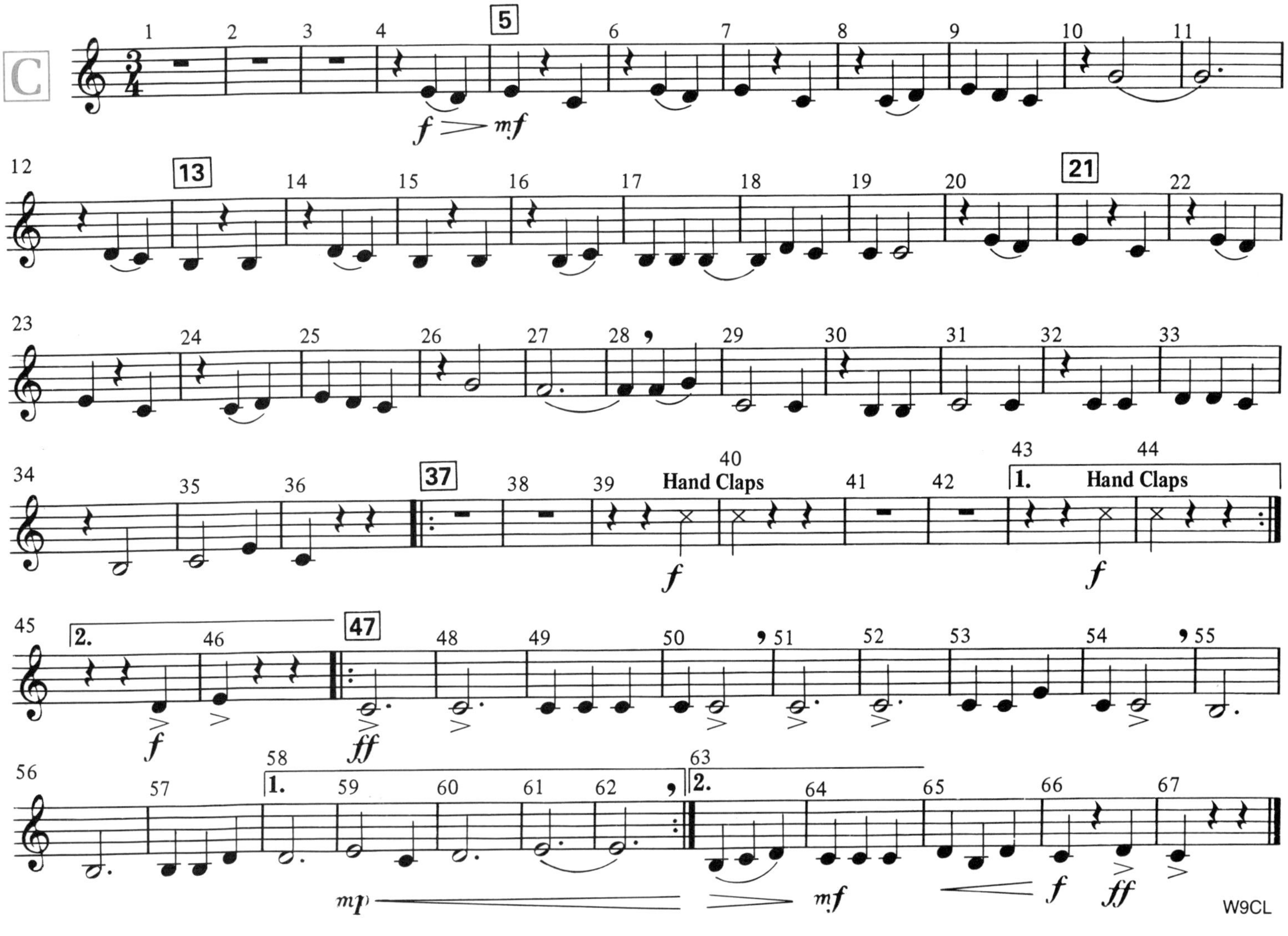

Manhattan Beach

John Philip Sousa

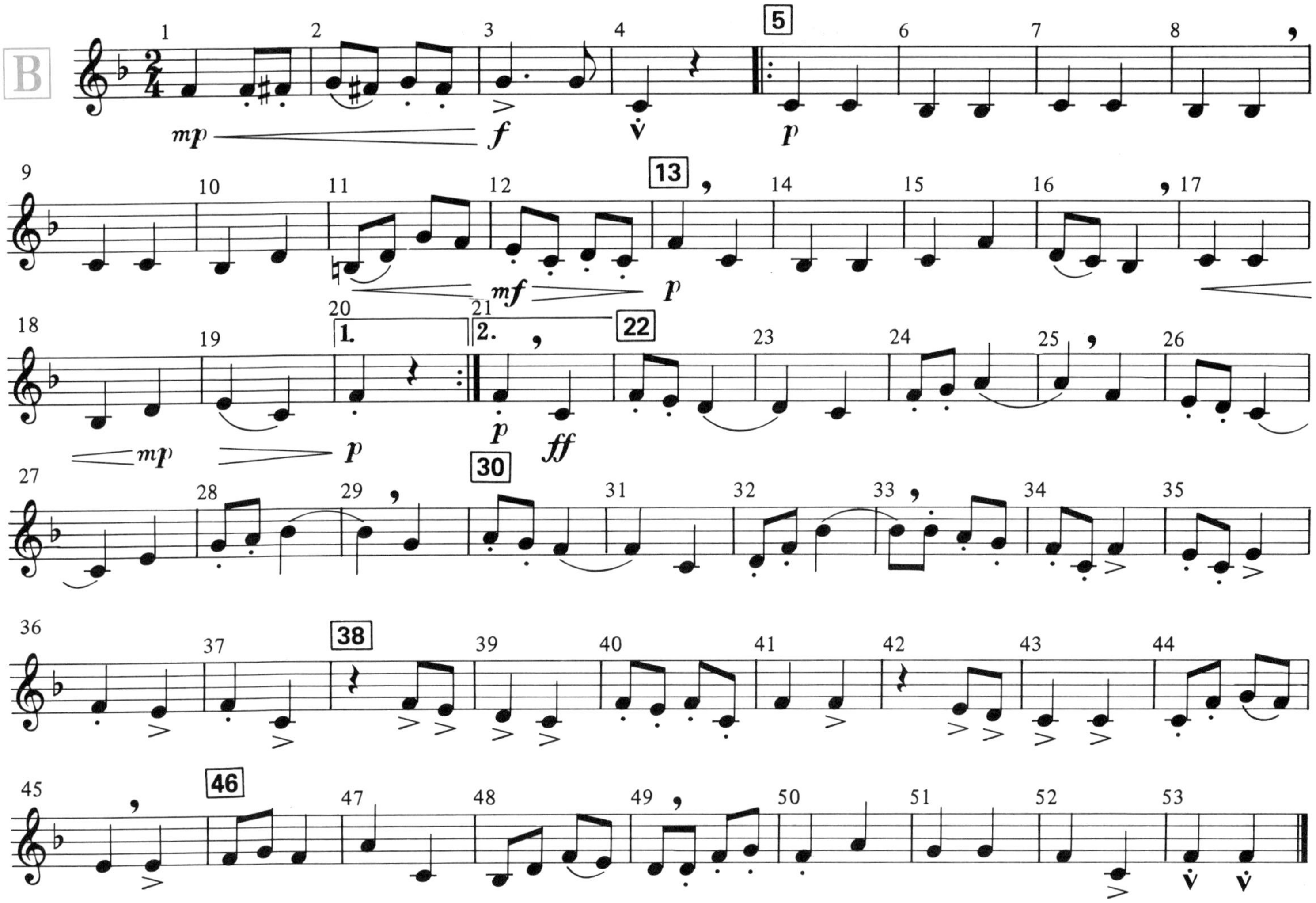
B

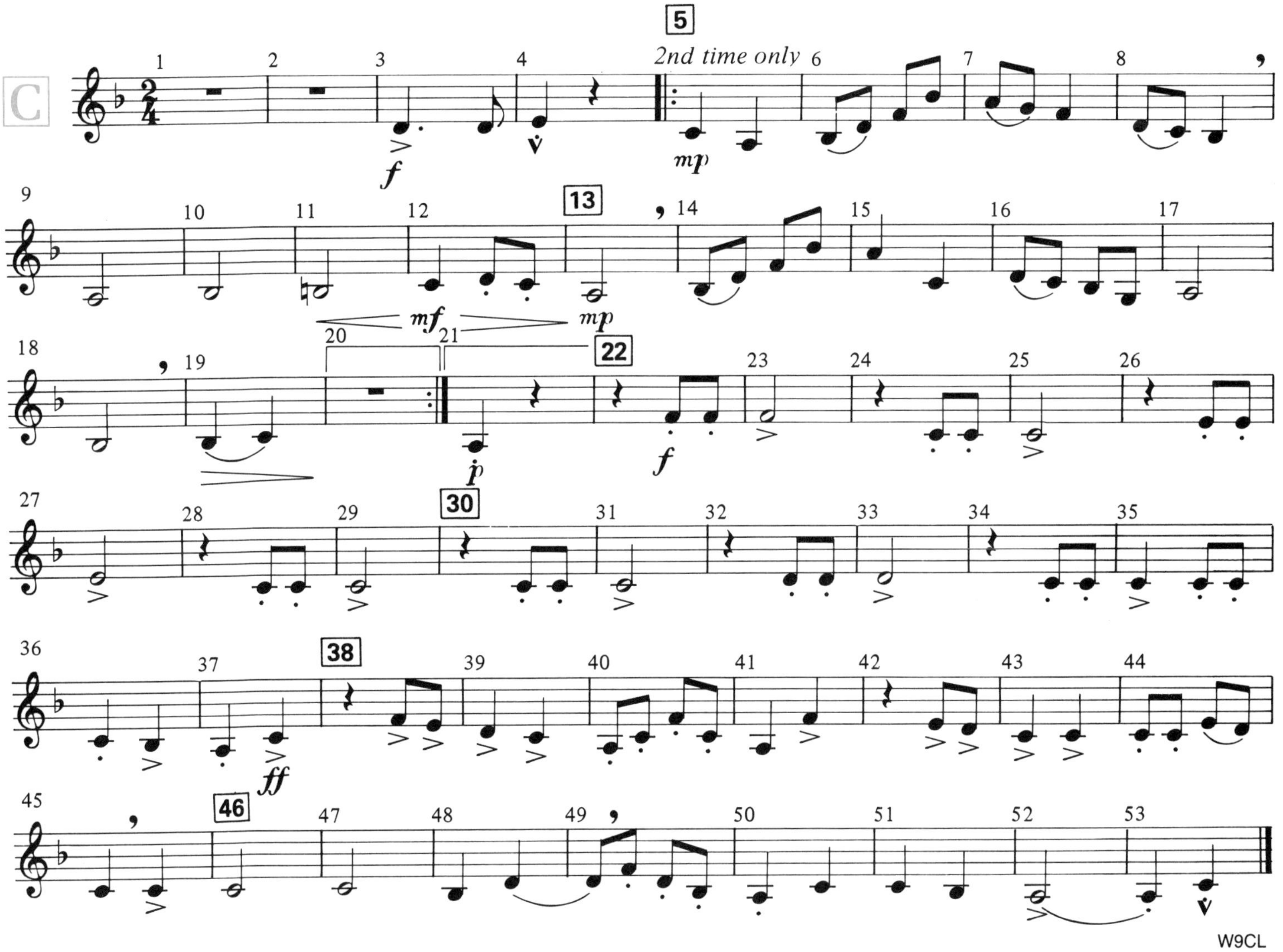
C
2nd time only

Minuet

J.S. Bach

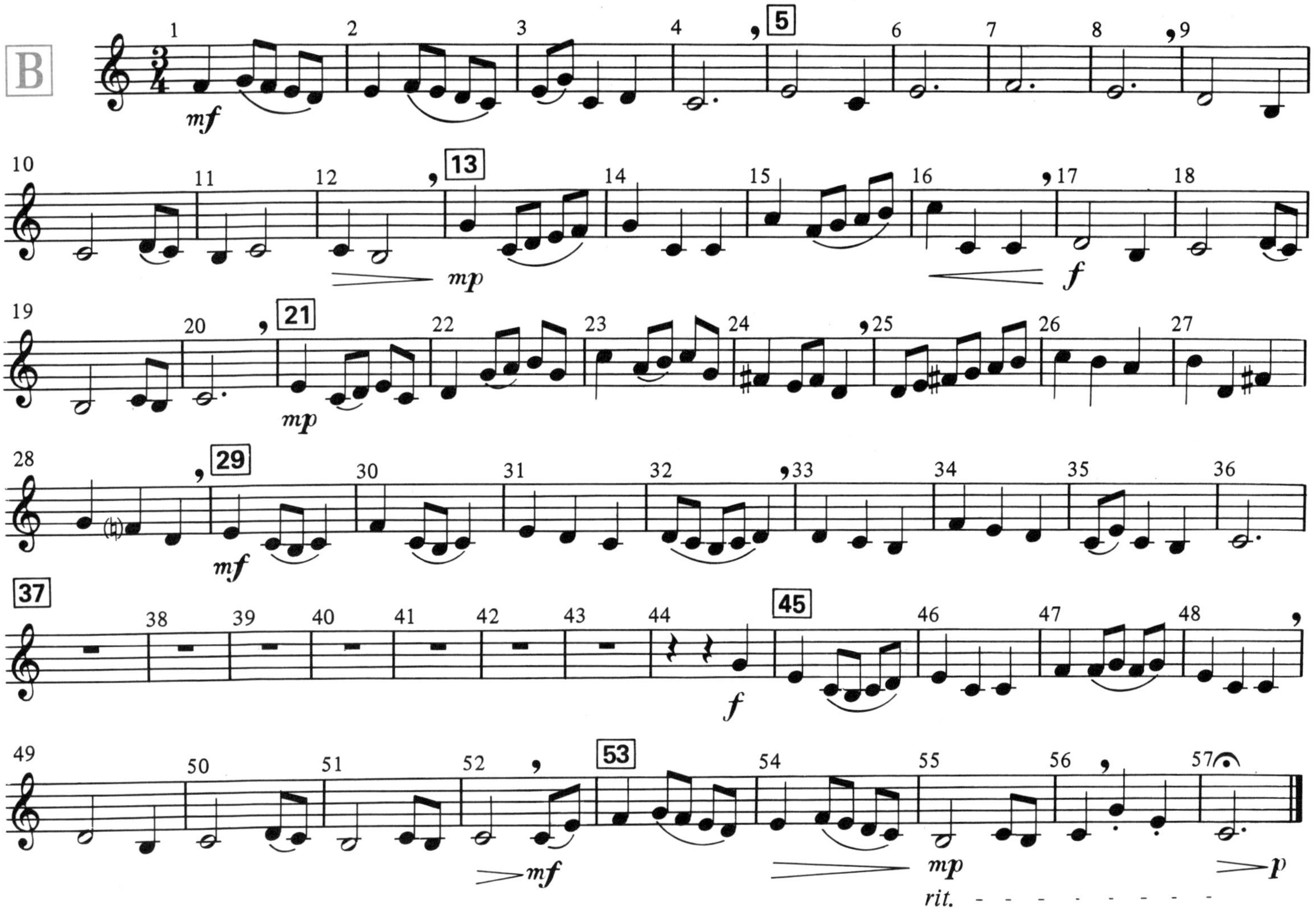
B
rit.

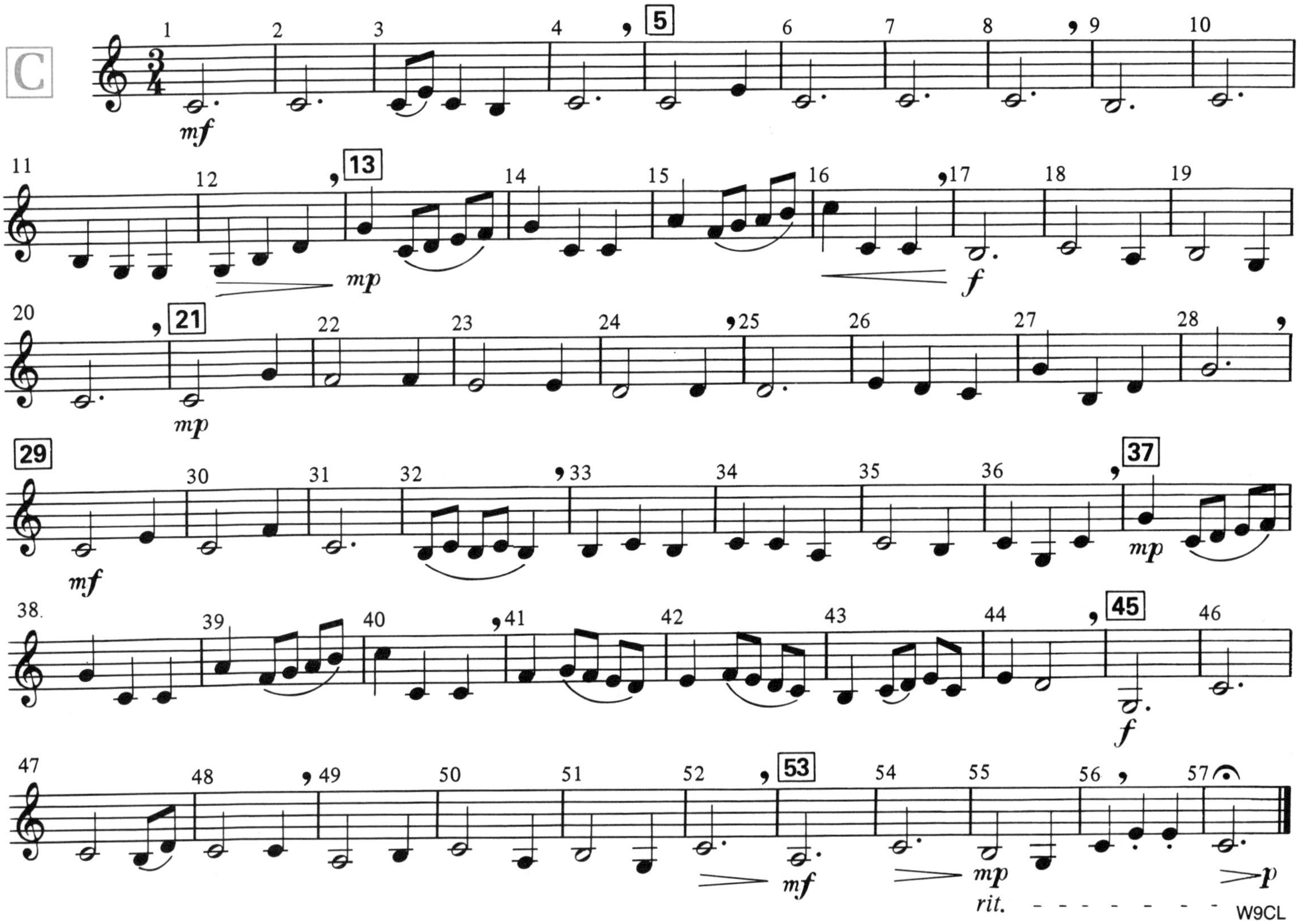
C
rit.

Ricochet Rock

Chuck Elledge

19

Hatikvah

Traditional Hebrew Song

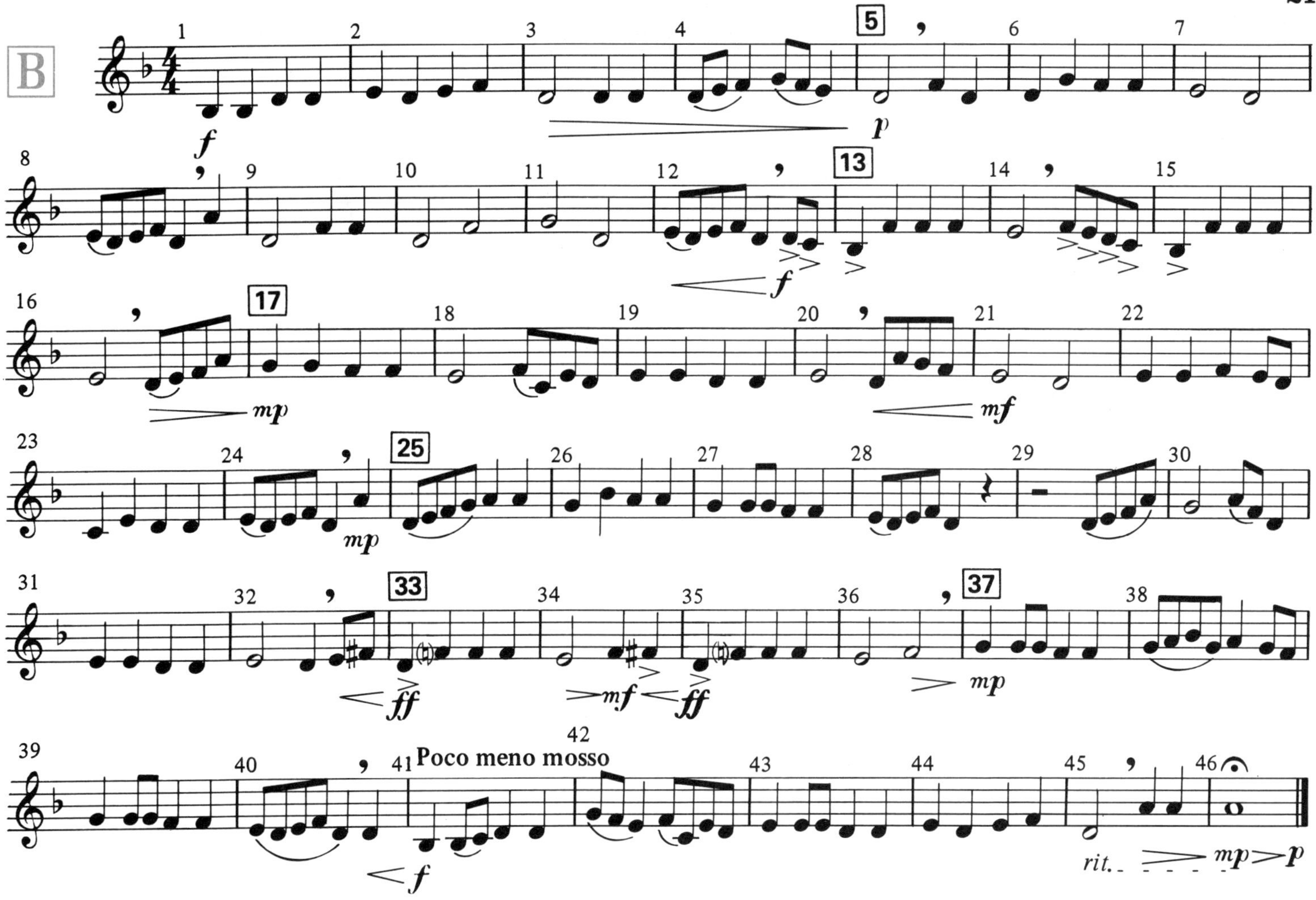
B
Poco meno mosso
rit.

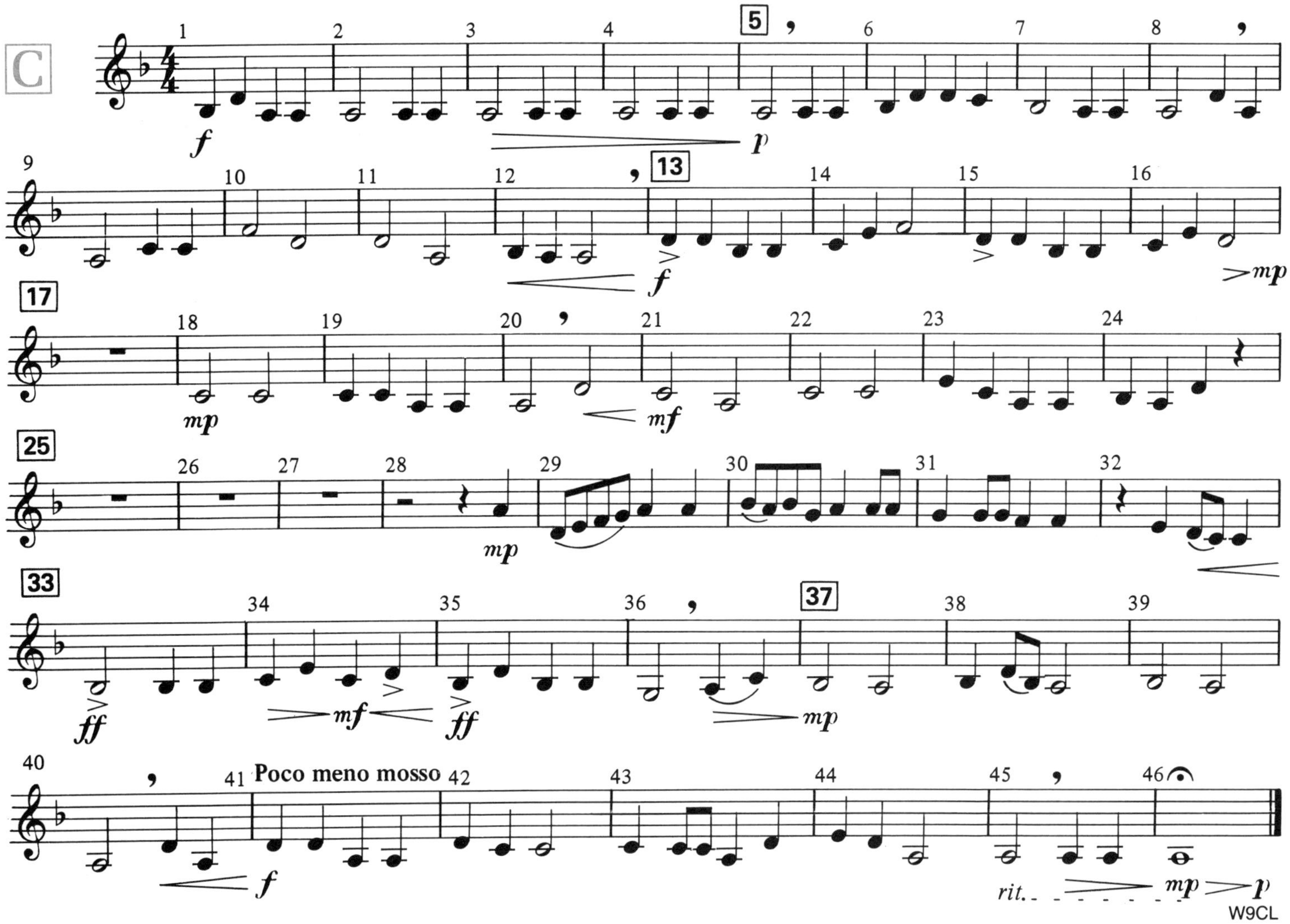
C
Poco meno mosso
rit.

When The Saints Go Marching In

Traditional

B

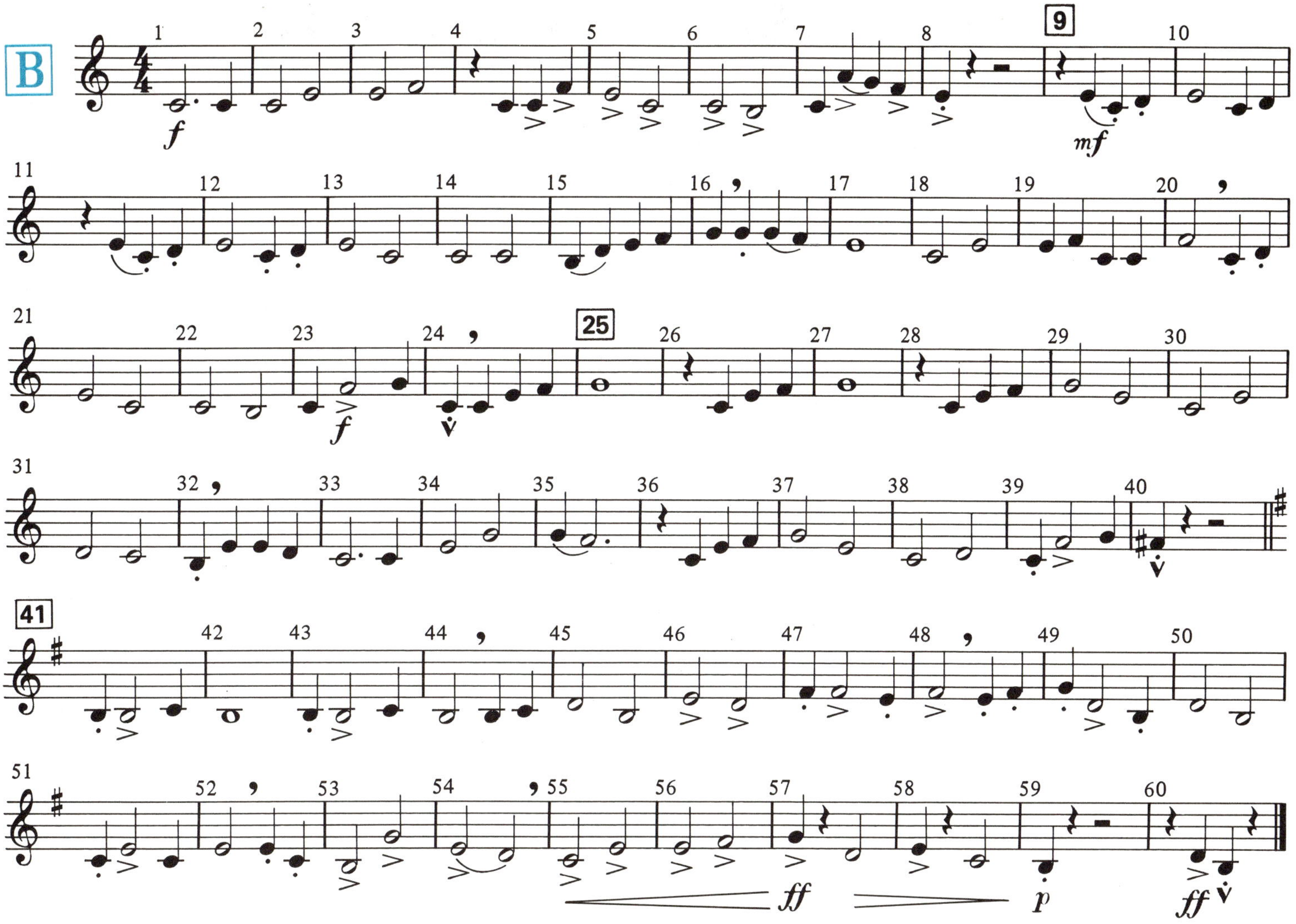

C

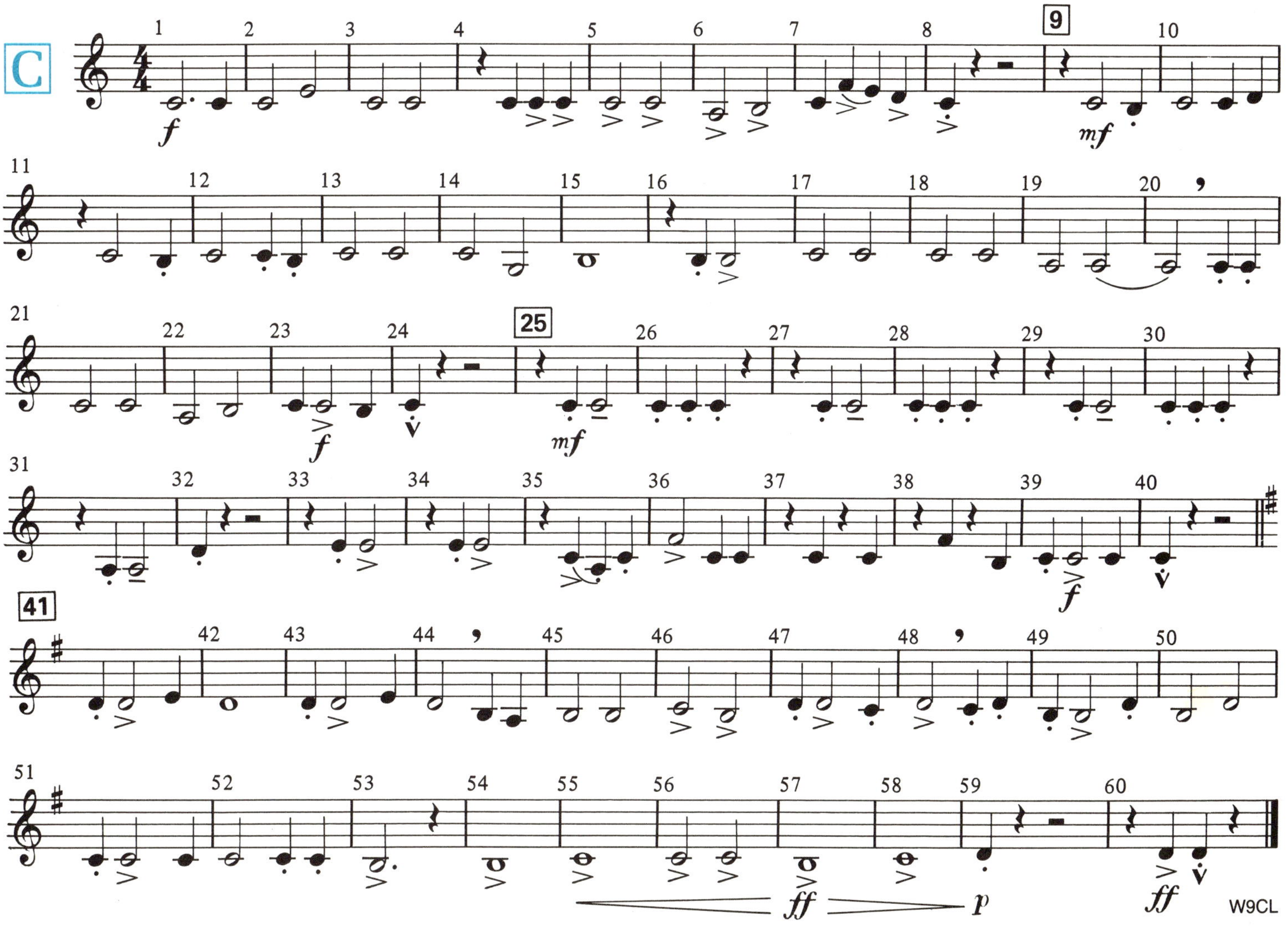

Performance Notes

Billboard March was originally composed in 1901 by John N. Klohr (1879-1956) and has since become a popular concert and circus march. Klohr, a vaudeville trombonist, dedicated the piece to *Billboard,* the entertainment newspaper. This arrangement features the familiar trio and break strain sections and makes a terrific opener for Showcase concerts and recitals.

The Conquering Hero is an excerpt from the third act of Georg Frideric Handel's epic oratorio *Judas Maccabaeus.* Handel (1685-1759) and his librettist Rev. Thomas Morell borrowed the melody and text of this famous choral composition from *Joshua,* another Handel oratorio, in 1747. Today, it is widely performed as an inspirational piece.

BINGO! is a traditional American folk song about a farmer and his dog. It has become a popular children's clapping and singing game, as the singers spell the dog's name, dropping one additional letter every time the verse is sung. This arrangement features several novelty percussion instruments.

The traditional American song **Simple Gifts** celebrates the pure and uncomplicated lifestyle of the Shakers, a community-oriented sect which flourished in New England and the Ohio River Valley in the early and mid-nineteenth century. Aaron Copland later borrowed the melody for his 1944 ballet *Appalachian Spring.*

Las Chiapanecas, a traditional Mexican folk song, praises the graceful dancing of the young women of Chiapas, a region of extreme southeastern Mexico. Chiapas is famous for its marimba music, and **Las Chiapanecas** was probably originally played on this mallet percussion instrument. The middle section has become the popular "Hand-Clapping Song" often performed at sporting events and other festive occasions.

Manhattan Beach March is one of John Philip Sousa's most popular marches. Sousa (1854-1932) was known as "The March King" for his nearly single-handed development of the march as a popular musical form in America. The march is named for a fashionable East Coast resort community where Sousa's band first played in 1893, the year the march was composed.

Johann Sebastian Bach (1685-1750) composed **Minuet** in 1720 and included it in a collection of short piano solos, the *Klavierbuechlein.* This collection was originally intended to be an instructional book for his bride Anna Magdalena, and has become the source of some of Bach's most famous melodies.

Ricochet Rock is an original blues-rock song by Chuck Elledge. The title refers to the way the melody rebounds off itself and ricochets between the different parts. This piece uses the familiar twelve-bar blues progression and features contemporary rhythms and harmonies.

Hatikvah ("The Hope") is the national anthem of Israel. The words, by Naftali Herz Imber (1856-1909), describe the deep longing in Jewish culture for reunification in the homeland. The exact origin of the melody is unknown, although it has been ascribed to Bedrich Smetana's symphonic poem *Vltava* and to nineteenth-century Sephardic cantors.

When the Saints Go Marching In is an American spiritual which has been adopted as a standard by Dixieland jazz musicians. James M. Black was legally credited with authorship of the song in 1896, and it immediately became popular in New Orleans and in the Caribbean islands. This arrangement features a dramatic key change before the last rousing "Dixie-style" chorus.